FOLENS IDEAS BANK TELLING STORIES

Louis Fidge

Contents

How to use this book	2	Trespassers Will Be Eaten!	26
Introduction	3	DIY Fairy Stories	28
Thinking About Stories and Story Telling		**Thinking About Plots**	
What Makes a Story?	4	Dreamtime	30
Remembering and Retelling Stories	6	Sequencing and Predicting	32
Traditional Tales	8	Stimulating Ideas	34
Steps to Telling Stories Orally	10	Under the Manhole Cover!	36
Thinking About Characters		Daring Deeds at Drakensberg	38
Thinking About Me	12	Extending the Story	40
The Bombshell	14	**Supporting The Writing Process**	42
Feelings	16	Steps to Becoming a Real Author	43
Things People Say	18	Story Planning Checklist	44
Characters as Story Starters	20	Story Planning Wheel	45
Thinking About Settings		Reviewing Checklist	46
Setting the Scene	22	Editing Checklist	47
The 'Secret' Club	24	Eight ways to help ...	48

Folens Publishers

How to use this book

Ideas Bank books provide you with ready to use, practical photocopiable activity pages for your children **plus** a wealth of ideas for extension and development.

TEACHER IDEAS PAGE   **PHOTOCOPIABLE ACTIVITY PAGE**

Clear focus to the activity.

Suggestions for developing work on the photocopiable pages.

Background information and other help given.

Extension activities suggested to take the work one step further.

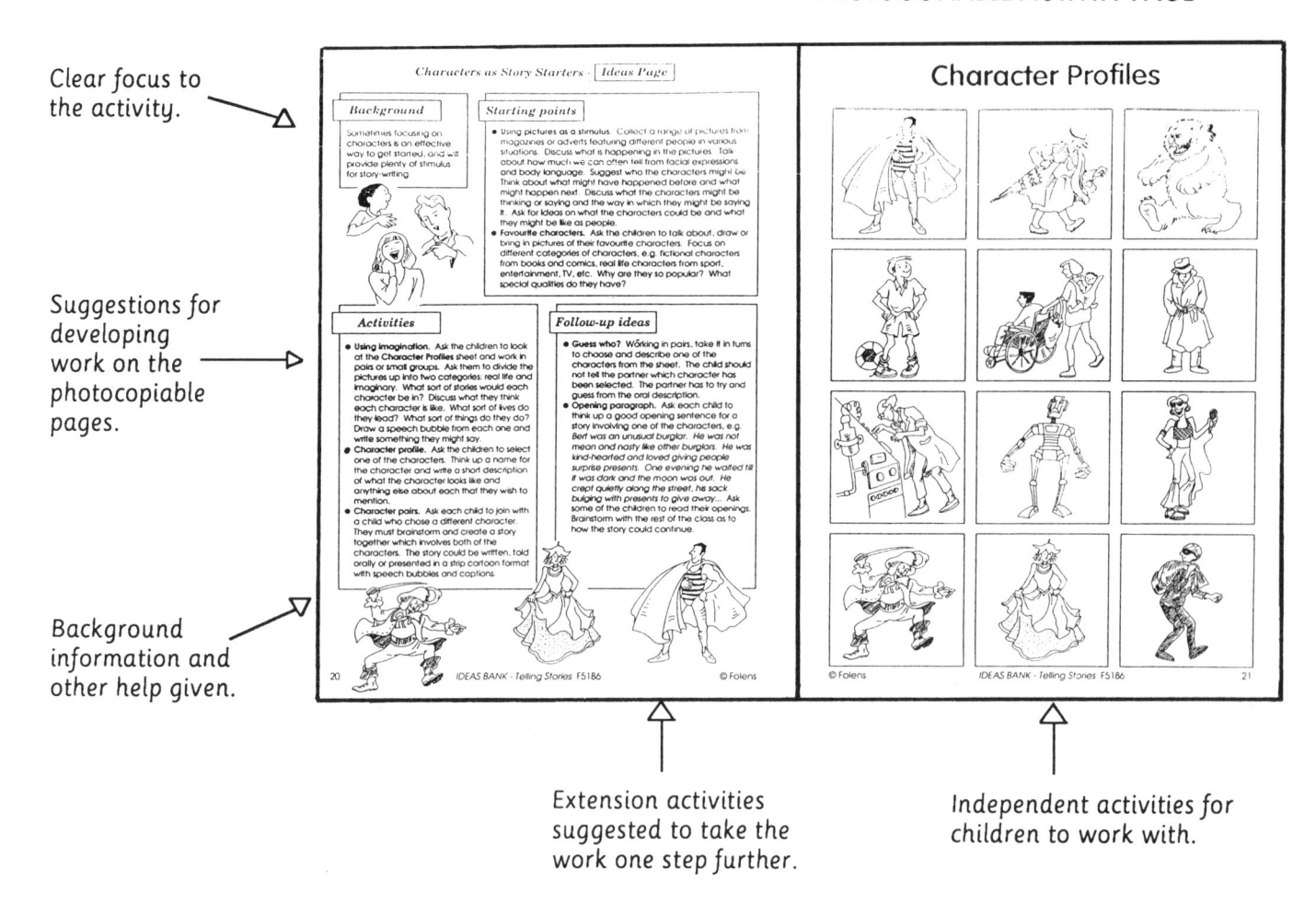

Independent activities for children to work with.

- Time-saving, relevant and practical, **Ideas Bank** books ensure that you will always have work readily to hand.

Acknowledgements

Folens books are protected by international copyright laws. All rights reserved. The copyright of all materials in this book, except where otherwise stated, remains the property of the publisher and author(s). No part of this publication may be reproduced, stored in a retrieval system, or transmitted, in any form or by any means, for whatever purpose, without the written permission of Folens Limited.

Folens do allow photocopying of selected pages of this publication for educational use, providing that this use is within the confines of the purchasing institution. You may make as many copies as you require for classroom use of the pages so marked.

This resource may be used in a variety of ways; however it is not intended that teachers or students should write into the book itself.

© 1993 Folens Limited, on behalf of the author.

Cover by: In Touch Creative Services Ltd.   Illustrations by: Helen Herbert.   Cover Photo © Bonnie Timmons (The Image Bank).

First published 1993 by Folens Limited, Albert House, Apex Business Centre, Boscombe Road, Dunstable, LU5 4RL, England.
ISBN 185276518-6

Printed in Singapore by Craft Print

Introduction

This *Ideas Bank* is designed to help children understand better the processes of story-writing and story-telling and to help them to become more effective in their own abilities to write and tell stories. It is not another bank of random ideas for creative writing.

It offers teachers and children a framework and structure for supporting the development of story-writing and story-telling skills. It offers a comprehensive range of stimulating activities for promoting written and oral story-telling and encourages children to reflect on the processes involved and the skills they are using.

The materials help children think about different styles and genres of stories. They involve them in generating their own ideas, planning, editing, drafting and thinking about presentation and audience. Throughout, children are frequently encouraged to collaborate, discuss and support each other in the writing process.

Synopsis of the sheets

- **Thinking About Stories and Story-Telling**

  - **What Makes a Story?** This considers what stories are and why people tell them. It encourages children to think about different types of stories and the important ingredients in them, i.e. settings, characters, events.
  - **Remembering and Re-telling Stories.** Children are asked to think about stories which are special to them and to re-tell them in their own words. They are also asked to reflect on what stories they themselves tell regularly.
  - **Traditional Tales.** The story of Little Red Riding Hood is used as a way of thinking about story-telling and story-writing.
  - **Steps to Telling Stories Orally.** Suggestions are made for stimulating oral story-telling, as well as providing a checklist for children, helping them to structure their thinking.

- **Thinking About Characters**

  - **Thinking about Me.** One way of encouraging children to think about characters is to think about a character they know best - themselves!
  - **The Bombshell.** This sheet offers story-writing opportunities based on the theme of 'Grans'.
  - **Feelings.** An important part of characterisation is being able to empathise with characters. On this sheet the focus is on peoples' feelings displayed by their actions and what they say, as well as by how they look.
  - **Things People Say.** The things people say and how they say them often tells us a great deal about the character concerned. Good use of dialogue in stories is an effective tool for the writer to develop.
  - **Characters as Story Starters.** Focusing on characters is often a good way of stimulating ideas for stories.

- **Thinking About Settings**

  - **Setting the Scene.** Here, the focus is on creating a good context for a story, starting from the familiar and stimulating the imagination.
  - **The 'Secret' Club.** The context of 'secret' societies and clubs is the starting point for this writing opportunity.
  - **Trespassers Will Be Eaten!** The giant's garden seems safe enough, until the giant returns home!
  - **DIY Fairy Stories.** Guided story-writing opportunities are offered, enabling children to create their own fairy story.

- **Thinking About Plots**

  - **Sequencing** and **Predicting and Stimulating Ideas.** This set of activities provides support for planning and creating storylines. Activities are included on picture sequences, using prediction, story starters and a comprehensive 'Events' starter web packed with ideas to get children started.
  - **Under the Manhole Cover!** The science-fiction theme of this sheet leads children into developing their own storylines around suggested plot ideas.
  - **Dreamtime.** The Aboriginal story about the creation of the world provides the basis of the storyline for this writing activity.
  - **Daring Deeds at Drakensberg.** Princess Starlight has been captured. Each child with their group of hand-picked comrades must plan to enter the Duke of Doom's castle at Drakensberg and attempt to rescue her!

- **Supporting the Writing Process**.

  - This collection of checklists and planning sheets may be used as *aides-mémoires* to help guide and structure children's thinking about the different processes involved in writing stories.

What Makes a Story? - Ideas Page

Starting points

- Discuss a selection of the following statements and questions in pairs, small groups or as a class.
  - Why do people tell and write stories?
  - Why do people listen to and watch stories?
  - What kinds of things do people tell stories about?
  - Why are stories written for, and told to, children?
  - Stories are important to people.
  - Stories 'belong' to everyone.
  - A story can only be 'proper' if it is written down.
  - Everyone can tell stories.
  - Stories are a waste of time because they are not true.
  - The best stories are true stories.
  - Stories may not be true but they can be 'real'.
  - You cannot learn anything from stories.

Activities

- Use the **What Makes a Story?** sheet. The following activities could be carried out individually but are best worked on in pairs or small groups to encourage discussion.
- Give children a copy of the sheet. Explain that it will help them think about different sorts of stories and the kinds of things that can be expected to be found in them.
- Discuss the fact that we can classify stories into different types, e.g. fairy stories, adventure stories, animal stories. Look at some illustrated book covers and ask what sort of stories they think these pictures represent.
- Explain that in most stories there are certain ingredients, e.g. characters, settings, events, plots.
- Look at the example given to ensure children understand the terms.
- Encourage the children to discuss their ideas and complete as much of the grid as they can.
- Use books in the classroom and think about books children have read.
- Review and discuss contributions from different groups as a class.
- Use the grid idea to make a large class chart incorporating all the best of their ideas. Illustrate it with pictures of some of the characters, settings and events mentioned. Add to the chart over time. More ideas will emerge, as certain categories will inevitably be missed, e.g. historical stories.

Follow-up ideas

- **Titles.** Talk about what titles of books can tell you about types of stories. Look at some book titles together. Make up a range of imaginary titles for different genres.
- **Pictures.** Show the children some pictures from some story books. Is it possible to tell what type of story book they come from? Design some jacket covers for different types of stories.
- **Favourite authors.** Which books have children read? How would they classify the books? What do they particularly like about the different authors?
- **Opening lines.** Is it possible to identify the type of story from just a paragraph. Read and discuss the characteristics of opening paragraphs? Do they make children want to read more? Think about the importance of a good opening. How might the story carry on? Make up some good opening sentences for different types of stories.
- **Book reviews.** Use the chart o help children think and talk about books they have read.
- **Class stories.** Every time you read a book to the children use the chart to help talk about the book. What type of story is it? Who are the main characters?
- **Stimulus for writing.**
  Encourage the children to refer to the chart to give them ideas and help them structure their thinking when planning and writing stories.

What Makes a Story?

TYPES OF STORY	TYPES OF SETTINGS	TYPES OF CHARACTERS	TYPES OF EVENTS
Fairy stories.	Castle, palace, woods, lakes.	King, Queen, Prince, Princess, dragon, frog, unicorn, witch, giant.	Magic spells, difficult challenges, getting lost, being captured and rescued, marriage, happy endings.

© Folens.   IDEAS BANK - Telling Stories F5186   5

Remembering and Retelling Stories - Ideas Page

Starting points

Stories I remember
- Ask the children what stories they remember being told when they were younger, e.g. by a parent or relative, teacher or on TV.
- Suggest each child makes a list of as many as they can remember.
- Compare their lists and discuss similarities and differences.
- In pairs, groups or as a class, retell some favourite stories.
- Discuss why children remember particular stories best. What makes them so special? Talk about who told them the stories and in what situations. Does the storyteller have anything to do with our remembering particular stories?
- Discuss the fact that most stories are still spoken rather than written down. We probably tell stories every day about:
  - ourselves and things that have happened to us
  - other people and what they have done
  - what has happened to them
  - things we have seen on TV
  - things other people have told us
  - stories in the news.

Stories I tell
- Ask the children to discuss the *I tell stories about...* chart and talk to each other about their responses. Ask each child to complete it individually. Are there any other categories that could be added? When complete, compare and discuss the outcomes. This idea has close links with **Thinking about Me** on page 12.

Activities

- **Retelling a traditional story.** Write down the names of several well-known stories on a board, e.g. *The Three Billy Goats Gruff Hansel and Gretel, Jack and the Beanstalk, Sleeping Beauty*.
  Divide the children into groups of about four. Ask each group to decide on one story and as a group retell the story, helping each other as they do so.
- **Retelling a story the children have read themselves.** Ask the children to retell a story they have recently read to a partner. Give the children some prior notice of this so that they can think about the task and prepare themselves. Explain that you want them to share their thoughts about how well their partner told the story, i.e. how much they understood, how clear the story was, how well it was presented.
- **Retelling a story the children have been read or told.** Read or tell an appropriate story to the class. Explain that you are going to ask them to recall it to each other afterwards. You may wish to discuss aspects of the story after you have finished as a way of drawing out the main points or explaining any difficult parts. In pairs, or small groups, ask the children to retell the story. Either ask for it to be done as a group effort, each contributing to the story as they go along, or for one child to retell the story to a partner or group. In this case the partner or rest of the group only help the individual out if he or she is in difficulty. The rest of the group then comment on how well remembered the content was and on aspects of presentation.

IDEAS BANK - Telling Stories F5186 © Folens.

Remembering and Retelling Stories

Name _____

I tell stories about ...

	A lot	Sometimes	Never
... myself			
... my friends			
... my family and relatives			
... arguments			
... TV			
... music			
... sport			
... holidays			
... school			
... sad things			
... funny things			
... frightening things			
... shopping			
... animals or pets			
... other things.			

© Folens. IDEAS BANK - Telling Stories F5186

Traditional Tales - Ideas Page

Background

Traditional tales provide a rich resource for developing story-writing. This idea focuses specifically on one traditional tale but it could be applied to many others.

Starting points

- **Recall and retell.** In groups, ask children to recall all they can about story of *Little Red Riding Hood*. Share ideas collectively as a class.
  Use the pictures to check the accuracy of recalled information and to retell the story. This presents an opportunity to discuss the art of successful story-telling. For example, what makes a good story-teller: expression? detail? acting it out? style of presentation?
- **Developing the story.** The pictures only select parts of the story. Ask children to flesh out the details.
  The ending has been left blank. Try to come to some consensus as to how the traditional story ends. The effect of the frightening nature of some tales on young children could be explored.
- Without conferring, ask individuals to make up an alternative ending. This could be drawn and/or written. In groups discuss some of these.
- **Considering the characters.** Discuss each character separately. Brainstorm children's thoughts and impressions of each character. What was he or she like? What did they think or feel at different points in the story? Write down adjectives or phrases on the board to describe them. As a follow-up, children could choose one character and write their own description.
  Take one or two of the pictures and discuss what each of the characters would be saying. Draw speech bubbles and write their words inside them to reinforce or teach the use of speech marks. Discuss how important it is in stories to know what people are thinking or saying.

Activities

Taking a different slant on the story

- Discuss how stories are sometimes told from one person's point of view. Little Red Riding Hood is traditionally shown as the 'goodie', whilst the wolf is the villain.
- Ask the children to write the story in first person form from the perspective of:
  a) Little Red Riding Hood, e.g. *My Gran lives in the woods. One day she was not very well so I decided to take some cakes and went to see her.*
  b) the wolf
  c) Gran
  d) the woodcutter.
- Read the finished versions to each other and discuss.
- Another, slightly more difficult, possibility is to try and think of writing a story with a similar theme, but changing the characters and setting. This would need more of discussion and support.
- The story lends itself well to a discussion of speech marks (see above). Ask the children to look in a variety of books and see if they can find different conventions for representing speech marks.
- Another idea is to use the story as a play and write it out as a play script, incorporating stage directions and prompts for characters.

Traditional Tales

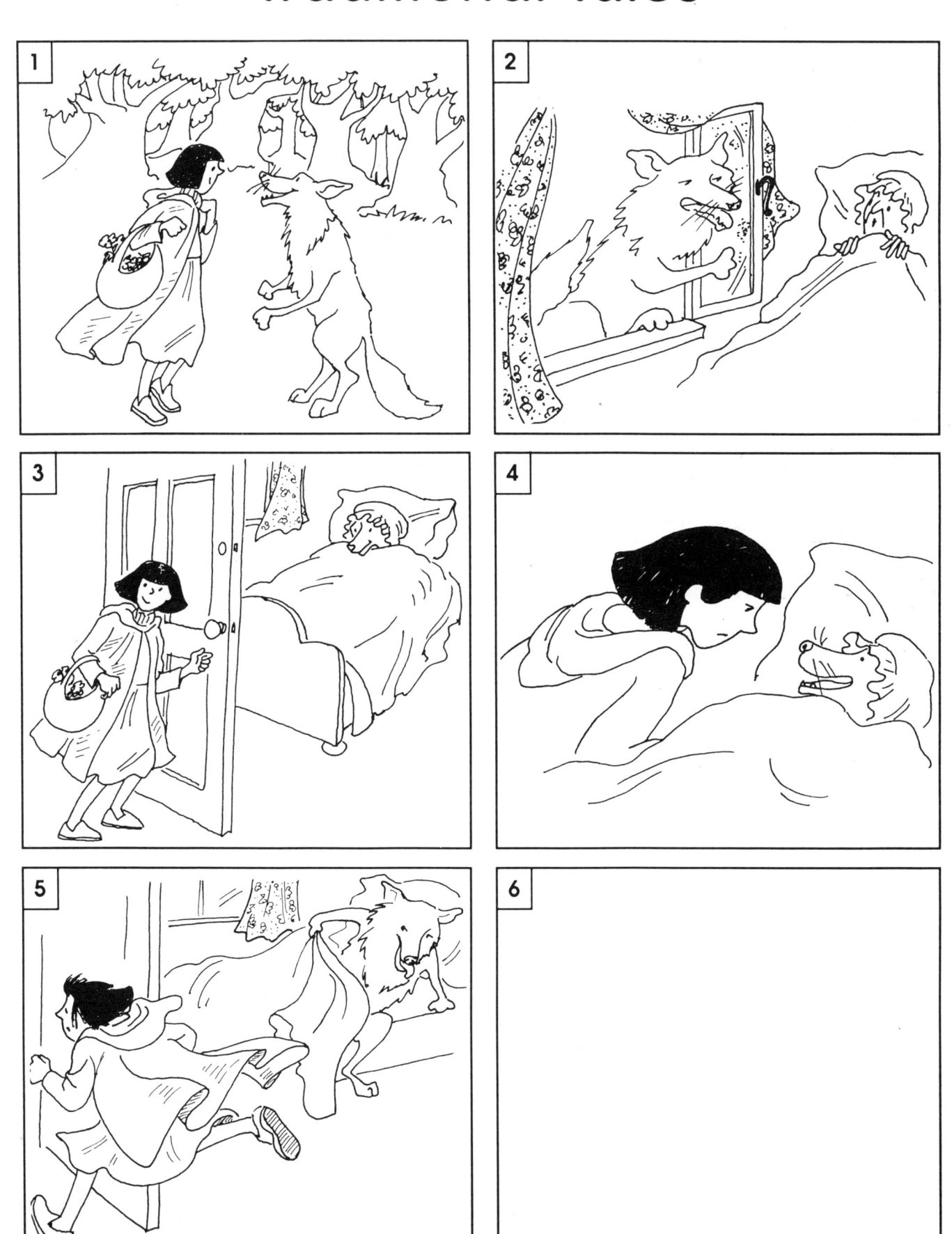

Steps to Telling Stories Orally - Ideas Page

Background

More emphasis is often placed on writing stories than on telling stories. Throughout this book opportunities are presented for talking about stories and encouraging anecdotal, personal talk. Discussion can be a part of the creative process in formulating ideas for stories and in reflecting on them - in pairs, small groups and as a class.

Activities

- **Involving children in story-telling.** The following ideas are all suggested as a way of encouraging oral story-telling, although each may of course also be developed into a story-writing opportunity if desired.
- **Chain stories.** Give a small group an opening sentence, paragraph or story beginning. The children then take turns to contribute to and finish the story (or keep it going as long as possible). Their attempts could be recorded and shared with a wider class audience.
- **Busy Pictures.** Give pairs of children (or small groups) an interesting picture. The children talk about what is happening, discuss what might have led up to events in the picture and predict what might happen next.
- **Picture sequences.** Provide the children with a set of six or so pictures which, when sequenced, tell a story. Each group has to confer and order the pictures into an appropriate sequence. Comparison of the outcomes of different groups often reveals variations which in themselves are productive to discuss. The group then develops and extends their story.
- **Objects.** Give each group a number of objects (depicted in pictures or words). Ask them to make up a collaborative story in which each of these objects features. Giving children a set of characters to weave into a story is variation on this activity.
- **Swap-a-story.** In pairs, ask the children to tell each other an amusing personal anecdote and then move on to retell their partner's story to someone else. A variation of this is for the teacher to divide the class into two large groups and to tell each half a different short story. Each child then partners a child from the other half of the class to swap stories.
- **Puppets, masks and cut-outs.** Have a collection of these in a story corner and encourage children to use them to help them make up and tell each other stories.
- **Reworking stories.** From a given story which has been read or told, it is possible to create many different story-telling opportunities. Children could:
  - invent an earlier episode or create a different ending
  - drop or add characters, or change a character's personality or behaviour in some way
  - change the context in which the story happens, e.g. the historical or geographical setting
  - tell the story from the points of view of the different characters
  - role play the story
  - imagine they are interviewing one of the characters from the story.

Follow-up ideas

Thinking about story-telling
- The teacher's example is very important to provide a model for the children to emulate. Inviting a professional story-teller into the school is another way of focusing discussion.
- Talk about what makes an interesting story-teller. Discuss ways of making stories come alive by using variations in voice (pitch, tone, expression), gestures and acting to dramatise points, eye contact and physical proximity.
- The **Steps to Telling a Story** checklist provides a useful way of helping children reflect on various aspects of story-telling and it provides a more structured way for children to develop their own personal story-telling skills.

Steps to Telling a Story

1 *Plan what your story will be about*

- It could be:
  - about something that happened to you or someone you know
  - based on a story you have seen or read
  - a story you make up.

2 *Get the story outline clear in your head*

- Be sure your story has a clear beginning, middle and end.
- Draw a few pictures to remind you of important events or ideas.

3 *Think about presentation*

- Decide whether you will:
  - sit or stand
  - use actions or mime
  - use different voices for different characters
  - record it and listen to it.

4 *Try it out with a partner*

- Discuss your performance with a partner.
- Think about ways of improving it.
- Decide on any changes that need to be made.

5 *Practise*

- Practise telling your story until you know it well.
  - to the mirror   - to your parents
  - to yourself).

6 *Perform*

- Tell your story to different audiences. This might be to a group, your class, younger children, your friends.)

Thinking About Me - Ideas Page

Background

Characterisation is an important aspect of story-telling.
We can learn about characters by various means:
- by describing the outward features, physical appearance and observable characteristics
- building up a character's profile - talking about what the character thinks, says and does, and the way in which the character behaves.

One way for children to think about characterisation is to ask them first to think about characters they know best.

Starting points

- **Everyone is different.** Talk about ways in which we are all different, e.g. age, gender, height, facial features, hair, ways of dressing, habits. Discuss the advantages and disadvantages of everyone looking alike. Discuss what other people notice when they look at you. Ask children to bring in photographs of themselves. Mask the eyes or the face below the eyes. Can children guess whose photo it is from the remaining clues?

- **Self-Portrait.** Ask children to look in a mirror carefully and draw a self-portrait. Write their names on the back. Make a display of the pictures. Next, ask each child to write a description of their observable physical features. Do not include names in the description. Make a display of the descriptions. Can the children match the description to the correct picture? Discuss how accurate each is. How could the descriptions be improved?

Activities

- **Everyone is special and unique.** Many different things contribute to making us what we are. Ask children to think about what sort of personal qualities they have. Brainstorm possible ideas, e.g. quiet, friendly, quick-tempered. Ask children to think of some things that make them different and special - some things they are good at, some things they are proud of, somewhere they have been or something they have seen, some of their favourite things. Write headings on a board to remind them. Ask them to jot down a few examples under each heading. Ask children to discuss what they have written with a partner and select from their draft notes ten things they would like others to know about them. Ask each child to write their name on their Personal Profile, label it and display it for all to see.

- **Memories.** Tell children a teacher-based anecdote about yourself. Ask children to work in pairs. Provide each pair with the 'Memories' sheet. Ask them to talk to each other about their memories. Afterwards, ask each child to choose one memory to write about. Make a class collection of *Memories*. Alternatively, ask each child to write about a memory their partner shared with them. Ask the partner to read it to see if it accurately reflected what they said.

Follow-up ideas

- **Personal anecdotal writing.** Suggest children tell each other about themselves and tell anecdotes and stories about their experiences, e.g. fears, dreams, pets, accidents, parties.

- **What would you do if ...?** Pose several 'What would you do if ...?' questions for discussion. For example - What would you do if ... you met a gorilla in the supermarket? ... you went shopping and found you had lost all the money your mum had given you? Discuss each scenario, talk about how the children would behave, what they would think or say and how they would feel. Consider a variety of possible outcomes for each. Use any of these as a stimulus for writing a short story about themselves finding in such a situation.

Memories

- Choose one of these to talk to your partner about.

I remember when I was really small...

I always remember going to the Safari Park...

- Some things you used to do when you were very young.
- Something very exciting that happened to you.

When I was younger, I hated going swimming...

I will never forget the day my pet gerbil died....

- Something that you can remember that worried you.
- Something you can remember that made you sad.

NOW
- Choose one to write about **or**
- write about another memory you have.

© Folens.   IDEAS BANK - Telling Stories F5186   13

The Bombshell - Ideas Page

Starting points

Read the start of **The Bombshell** together.
- **Gran.** Discuss the children's impressions of Gran. What sort of character is she? How would they describe her? What do they think she looks like? Perhaps they could try to draw her. Write a class description of her from the children's comments. What do you think Meg and her Mum think of her? Ask the children to comment on what they think she would say about different things, e.g. the TV, Meg's hair. Suggest some different situations, e.g. on a crowded bus without a seat and ask how they think Gran would behave. Is Gran **all** bad? Ask the children to try to explain **why** she might behave as she does. Ask them to think of some good qualities she might have.
- **Meg.** Discuss Meg in a similar way. Perhaps they could write their own descriptions of how they imagine her to be. How does she feel about Gran? Do they have any impressions of where she lives or what her house is like? What do they think of Meg's Mum so far? What is she like? Do they have any other ideas about people (or pets) who might live with Meg?
- **The Bombshell.** Talk about how Meg felt when she heard the news. Discuss why Meg's Mum might be going into hospital. Talk about why she asked Gran, and not someone else, to stay. Is Meg an only child? Does she have a father?

Activities

- **Finish the story.** In small groups ask the children to discuss how the story might continue. What sort of things would Gran say and do - about bedtimes, washing, cleaning the house, school, TV, shopping? Would she be any different alone with Meg? How would Meg react? Share some of the children's thoughts together.
- **Strip cartoon.** The children could draw several picture frames of incidents at different times, telling the story of the next two days. They could draw speech bubbles showing some of the conversations that take place.
- **Gran changes.** Another possibility is to ask the children to think of and write about some incident which changes Gran's whole attitude to Meg. Perhaps a burglar tries to break in and Meg bravely deals with him. Perhaps there is a fire.
- **My Gran.** How does the Grandparent in the story compare with the children's Grandparents? Ask them to discuss the sort of person their Gran (or Grandad - or if this is not possible, an aunt or uncle) is. What sort of things does she/he say and do? How often do they see her/him? What does he/she look like? How does she dress? Ask them to write about a particular incident they can remember that gives a typical picture of their Grandparent.

Follow-up ideas

- **Super Gran.** Ask the children to imagine that their Gran had a very special quality, e.g. she could see what people were thinking, she was able to fly, she could run as fast as an express train. Ask them to talk about and make up some Super Gran stories.
- **My family.** Ask the children to produce brief descriptions of different members of the family. If necessary, provide simple headings to help them structure their thinking, e.g. how they look, personality, interests, irritating habits, things they always say.
- **Guess who?** Think of someone who works in the school. Do not tell anyone who it is. Write a description of him or her. See if others can guess from the description.
- **An imaginary person.** Ask the children to make up an imaginary character. For example, he or she could be a practical joker, be argumentative and unpleasant, be accident-prone. Invent a name for the person and character profile. Invent a short story featuring the character, e.g. *Mr Awful is mean and bad-tempered. He is always frowning and never smiles. He is very short-tempered, especially first thing in the morning. The other day he ...*

The Bombshell

Read the start of this story. Talk about what the 'bombshell' is.

I took a deep breath, fixed a smile on my face and entered the lion's den. My mum looked up. She was obviously pleased at the diversion my entrance caused. 'Hello Meg. Have you had a good day at school? Your Gran's here.' Before I could reply, Gran's piercing eyes bored into me and sent a shiver down my spine. It was just as if she could see right through me and read my every thought.

'Just look at the state of you Meg! What have you been doing? You look like you've been dragged through a hedge backwards. That's no way for a young lady to look,' she said.

I knew the only way to stop Gran going on was to change the subject. 'Hello Gran, how are you today?' I asked.

'Oh my arthritis is terrible! I can hardly bend or walk five yards. The pain is awful,' she whined. Gran was always moaning about her health.

I put my school bag on the table. That was a mistake! Gran immediately pounced on my exercise book which was poking out and launched into a full-scale attack.

'Don't they teach you anything at school these days. Your writing is worse than a scribble. And how you manage to make your book look so scruffy I'll never know.'

It was then that Mum exploded her bombshell. 'By the way Meg, I have to go into hospital for two days for a small operation. I didn't want to worry you so I haven't said anything before. Gran has come to stay and look after you.'

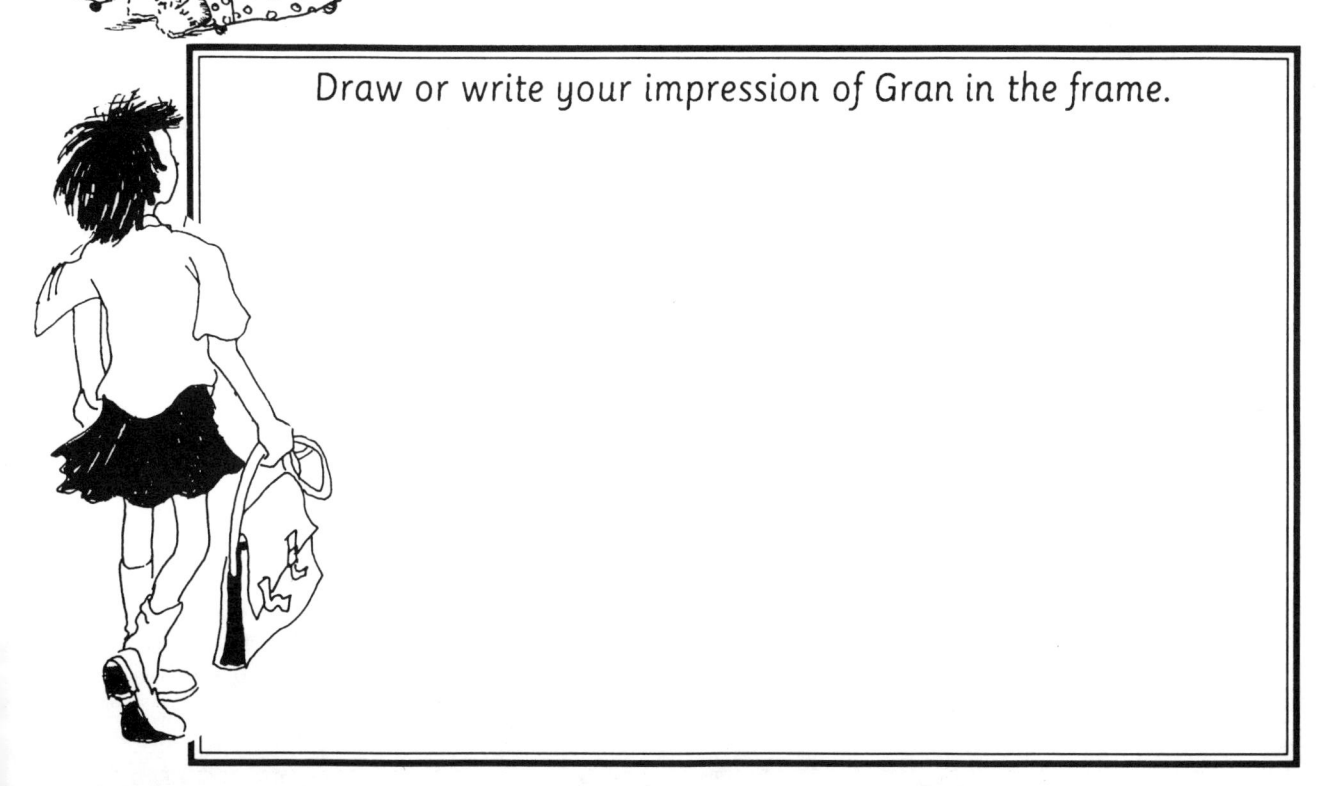

Draw or write your impression of Gran in the frame.

Feelings - Ideas Page

Starting points

- **Talk about feelings.** Take time to discuss characters and their feelings whenever you read a class story or passage from a book. Discuss how the various characters felt in particular situations and what made them feel this way.
- **List poems.** Brainstorm feelings in groups, encourage the children to share ideas as possible to share. Note down their ideas in rough. Create some simple list poems together on the board related to different feelings, e.g:

   Happiness is finding all the red jelly babies in a bag
   Happiness is ...

Activities

- **Feelings sheet.** Look at the *Feelings* activity sheet together. Talk about the sorts of things that make children feel: fed up, excited, etc. Think about other feelings that are not covered on the page, e.g. happy, surprised, sorry, spiteful. Ask each child to choose two more feelings and fill in the two blank spaces.
- **Reacting to feelings - doing.**
  Ask the children to write a sentence in each box about something they might do if they had that feeling, e.g. If I was excited I would not be able to sit still.
- **Reacting to feelings - saying.**
  Ask the children to write something they might say in each box if they had that particular feeling, e.g. If I was bored I would sigh and say 'I wish I was out playing with my friends.' Dialogue could be written in speech bubbles.

- **Reacting to feelings - looking.** Ask children to draw how they might look if they were experiencing the different feelings mentioned. Each box could be filled in with a small picture. This would need some discussion and some examples drawn on the board. We can usually tell a great deal from non-verbal clues. Body language - facial expressions, use of hands-tells us a great deal about feelings.

Follow-up ideas

- **Feeling blue?** We sometimes associate colours with particular feelings, e.g. red for anger, green with envy. Ask children to think about each of the feelings shown on the *Feelings* sheet and choose what they think is a suitable colour or pattern for each. Colour in the boxes appropriately. Ask the children to discuss their choices with each other and explain why they chose them. Perhaps they could make up a sentence or two about each. For example, *'When my sister turned off my favourite TV programme without asking I got mad. I got angry. I felt my mind bubbling up like a volcano. Red and yellow lightning flashes and stars blazed in my mind, blotting out everything else. I couldn't think straight. I couldn't control my feelings. I ...'*
- **A time when I felt ...** Focus on one of the feelings mentioned. Ask the children to write about a time when they experienced this feeling in their own lives. Help them structure their thinking:
  - Characters: Who was involved?
  - Context: Suggest that they write about the situation that gave rise to the feeling. When did it occur? Where?
  - Action: What happened? How did different characters behave? What did they do? What was said?
- **Tell a tale.** Write a list of a dozen or so different characters on the board, e.g. a policeman, a wizard, an astronaut. Work in pairs or threes. Ask the children to pick two or three characters. Then ask them to select two or three of the different feelings from the *Feelings* sheet. They could then write a short story involving the characters and the feelings chosen.

Feelings

frightened	jealous	angry
excited	bored	brave
lonely	curious	surprised
spiteful		

Things People Say - Ideas Page

Background

The activity sheet provides a novel way for children to experiment with dialogue and create different characters as a stimulus to story-telling and story-writing. The faces may be used in a variety of ways to support and complement many of the suggested activities below. Paste the sheet on to card to give the character more strength, before cutting out and assembling.

Activities

- **Using single pictures.** Present the children with a variety of pictures showing two characters in different situations, e.g. the police at the scene of a crime, a highwayman holding up a stage coach, a cartoon picture. Ask children in pairs to talk about what is happening, who the characters are, what they would be saying, how they would be feeling. Share their thoughts with other groups. This could be developed into a writing opportunity by imagining what happened before or predicting how things will continue.
- **Picture sequences.** Give children a sequence of pictures which tell a story or part of a story. Speech bubbles could be used to indicate when characters are speaking. Comic strips with the speech in the bubbles blanked out is good for this. Ask children to discuss the characters and what they might be saying. This could easily be turned into a story-writing activity.
- **Set the scene.** Describe an imaginary situation, e.g. two cavemen out hunting a sabre-toothed tiger suddenly come across one at a watering hole; astronauts about to set foot on an unexplored planet for the first time; planning a practical joke on a friend. Suggest the children role play the situation or use the character cut-outs. Develop the ideas into stories.

Starting points

- **Favourite sayings.** Do different people have favourite sayings? Talk about some of them.
- **People I know.** Create situations for children to role play or imagine the ensuing conversations, e.g. they are having great fun playing in the muddy garden (skidding on bikes, tunnelling, etc.). What sort of things would they say to each other? Their mother comes out and sees the mess. How does she react? What does she say?
- **It all depends.** Discuss the fact that we talk to people in different ways, depending on who they are. Think of the sort of conversation children might have: asking a friend for a sweet; taking a toy they want to play with from a younger brother; replying to a question from a visitor about their school.
- **Using story books.** Look for examples of dialogue in books. Discuss the way the characters talk to each other and what this tells us about the characters. Talk about the sorts of things they say and the way in which they might say things, e.g. their expressions, tone of voice. Think about the situations in which the conversations are taking place and how this affects what is said. Draw attention to the conventions used in writing down speech.

Follow-up ideas

- **Telephone conversations.** Provide the children with some situations in which they have to make a telephone call. Imagine the ensuing conversation. Use the ideas as beginnings (or middles) of stories. For example, children are out with a friend who gets his/her head stuck in some railings. They telephone for help.
- **Overhearing snippets.** Children overhear a snippet of a conversation on a bus outside the bank, which leads on to exciting things!
- **Disagreeing.** Think about different ways of agreeing and disagreeing. Role play situations (or use character cut-outs) involving themselves with different characters, in different situations, disagreeing over something. Discuss ways children would respond and the different kinds of language they would use.

Things People Say

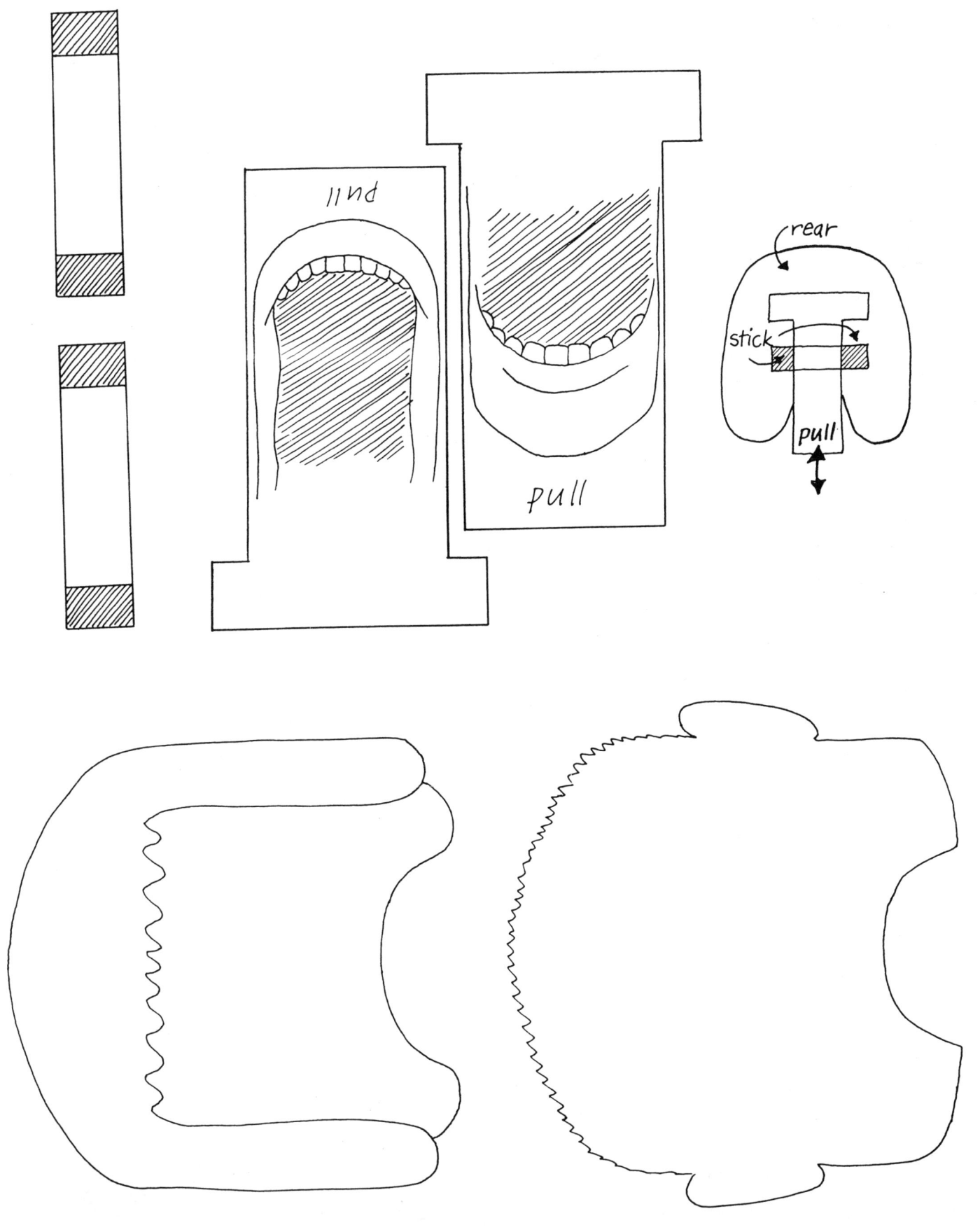

pull

pull

rear

stick

pull

© Folens.   IDEAS BANK - Telling Stories F5186   19

Characters as Story Starters - Ideas Page

Starting points

Sometimes focusing on characters is an effective starting point and will provide plenty of stimulus for story-writing.

- **Using pictures as a stimulus.** Collect a range of pictures from magazines or adverts featuring different people in various situations. Discuss what is happening in the pictures. Talk about how much we can often tell from facial expressions and body language. Suggest who the characters might be. Think about what might have happened before and what might happen next. Discuss what the characters might be thinking or saying and the way in which they might be saying it. Ask for ideas on what the characters could be and what they might be like as people.
- **Favourite characters.** Ask the children to talk about, draw or bring in pictures of their favourite characters. Focus on different categories of characters, e.g. fictional characters from books and comics, real life characters from sport, entertainment, TV, etc. Why are they so popular? What special qualities do they have?

Activities

- **Using imagination.** Ask the children to look at the **Character Profiles** sheet and work in pairs or small groups. Ask them to divide the pictures up into two categories: real life and imaginary. What sort of stories would each character be in? Discuss what they think each character is like. What sort of lives do they lead? What sort of things do they do? Draw a speech bubble from each one and write something they might say.
- **Character profile.** Ask the children to select one of the characters. Think up a name for the character and write a short description of what the character looks like and anything else about each that they wish to mention.
- **Character pairs.** Ask each child to partner a child who chose a different character. They should brainstorm and create a story together involving both characters. The story could be written, told or presented in a strip cartoon format with speech bubbles and captions.

Follow-up ideas

- **Guess who?** Working in pairs, children take turns to choose and describe one of the characters on the activity sheet. The child should not tell the partner which character has been selected. The partner should guess from the oral description.
- **Opening paragraph.** Ask each child to think of a good opening sentence for a story involving one of the characters, e.g.

Bert was an unusual burglar. He was not mean and nasty like other burglars. He was kind-hearted and loved giving people surprise presents. One evening he waited till it was dark and the moon was out. He crept quietly along the street, his sack bulging with presents to give away...

Ask some of the children to read their openings. Brainstorm with the rest of the class as to how the story could continue.

Character Profiles

Setting the Scene - Ideas Page

Background

A setting, a place, or an object can be a stimulus to creating and writing a story. A single picture can often stimulate a chain of ideas and lead to all sorts of writing opportunities, given guidance and structure. The following example shows how to start with a simple familiar setting and gradually lead children to think divergently and imaginatively about different possibilities, stimulating discussion and further response.

Starting points

- **The door.** Ask children to picture a door in their minds and describe it: colour, type of fittings, etc. Most will start from the familiar.
- **Using the imagination.** Is the door old or new? Wooden? Does it creak or open smoothly? What sort of building does it belong to? Is it a flat door in a modern multi-storey block? An old oak door from a thatched cottage? A castle door? A palace door? Who lives there? Is it in the past or the future?
- **A knock at the door.** Is it a gentle tap or someone hammering at it? What do they want? Perhaps the door opens upon a new and different world or an escape route for someone being chased. Where does it lead to? Is it a jail or a space-ship door?
- **Developing the idea.** Allow children to suggest other ways of developing the idea. Ask them to discuss things in small groups and note down other ideas. These could be used as a basis for planning a story, perhaps collaboratively in pairs or as a group, or perhaps just writing an exciting opening paragraph.
- **Presentation.** Children can draw their door on an A4 sheet of paper. This can be pasted onto another A4 sheet of paper down the left-hand side and folded so that it opens like a door. The story can then be written on the second sheet of paper. When the door is opened it reveals the story.

Activities

Using the activity sheet:

- Concentrate on one picture at a time. Focus on the known and observable. Ask the children to talk about what they can see. Discuss what they would hear and smell. What sort of people might they see there? What might they be doing? How would they feel if they were there?
- Gradually begin to use the picture to work on the children's imaginations. For example, imagine they see ... a shadowy figure lurking in the half-built house, dropping a mysterious-looking package into a hole. Imagine they hear ... a scratching sound coming from under the tipper truck, a low moaning noise from behind the bush. Use lots of 'What would you do if ...?' questions. Elicit the answers from the children. For example, what would you do if ... the machines on the building site suddenly took on the semblance of monsters, a slimy hand reached out from the murky depths of the lake and grabbed their ankle?
- Ask the children to invent some unexpected things that could happen. Ask them to change the time perspective, e.g. suppose it was a million years ago, or the year 2100. What would the museum/building site/school be like at night when there is no-one around?
- In pairs or small groups, brainstorm ideas for each picture along the lines suggested above. Suggest the groups share their thoughts and ideas. Use these to create oral or written stories.

Follow-up ideas

- Link two or three pictures together to write a story. The story must include these settings and the action should revolve around them.
- Ask the children to bring in pictures of different settings and build up a resource bank of them.
- Brainstorm and list as many different settings as possible. Use these to stimulate story ideas.

Setting the Scene

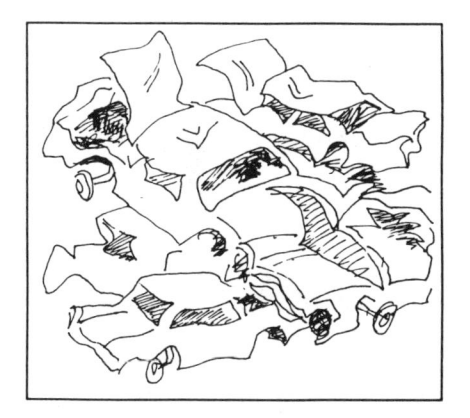

The 'Secret' Club - Ideas Page

Background

Stories of the *Black Hand Gang* and *Just William* genre are popular because they are full of action and adventure. These often involve a group of children outsmarting adults, have story-lines children can relate to, and are within the realms of possibility and everyday experience.

Starting points

- **Organised clubs.** Discuss experiences of belonging to organisations such as Cubs or Brownies. Talk about their distinctive features, e.g. specific meeting place, uniform, leaders, rules, symbols, rituals/routines and activities. Children could share anecdotes of fun, adventures and outings, orally or in written form.
- **Secret clubs.** Read stories of the *Famous Five* type. Are there any similarities with more formally organised clubs or groups? Who are the members? Are they always friends? Do they ever argue? Do they meet anywhere special, have a leader, have any rules? Discuss the use of secret symbols, codes and rituals. Have fun making up some codes and sending messages. What sort of adventures do the characters have?
- **Experiences of secret clubs/fellowships.** Who do children spend a lot of time with? It might be just a special friendship with one other person. Discuss any secret clubs they have been part of. Do they have a 'secret' meeting place? Are the members the same age and gender? What if someone else wanted to join? What sort of things do they talk about and do?

Activities

- **Setting the scene.** In small groups of four or five ask the children to brainstorm some ideas. Imagine they were forming a secret club.
  - What would they call their club or gang?
  - Design a symbol or badge for it. Discuss how it might reflect their interests or be related to their chosen name.
  - Decide on a good meeting place. Do they know of any - in their house, bedroom, attic, shed, somewhere else? What are the advantages and disadvantages of each? How could they prevent people interrupting their meetings?
  - Think of a password so only members could get in.
  - What rules would they need?
  - List the sorts of activities they would get involved in, e.g. midnight feasts, exploring, tracking, neighbourhood watch, sports, camping weekends, putting on shows.
  - Come together again as a class and share ideas.
- **The adventure.** Explain that they are now members of a secret club. Working in pairs, discuss and plan an adventure the group could have, based on some of the ideas already mentioned. Think about where it would take place, who would be involved in it, what sort of things would happen. Write it either collaboratively or individually. Afterwards, share, discuss and comment on each others' stories in groups with other members of their 'secret' club.

Follow-up ideas

- Each group could combine their stories into their own book of adventures. Further stories could be written and added to the book. **Spy stories.** The gang notice a suspicious-looking character and decide to follow her. She drops a package into a hollow tree in the park; meets another mysterious stranger. **Crime stories.** The gang observe someone breaking into a house; interrupt a bank robbery; see a mugging. **Disaster stories.** The day the gang saves the school from being burnt to the ground; rescues the old lady stranded by a flood.
- Children could also invent a whole new set of characters and write stories about a fictional group of children in a different setting or period of time, using the *Famous Five* idea.

The 'Secret' Club

Our Name

Password

Club Members

Membership Rules

Club Badge

Activities

Our Meeting Place

Trespassers Will Be Eaten! - Ideas Page

Background

The focus here is on giants, taken out of their traditional fairy tale setting and placed in a modern setting. This literary style is one frequently used by childrens' authors in which elements of the extraordinary intrude upon a 'normal' context and anything can happen, as in stories like *Peter Pan*. Ghost stories, dragons and lions with mystical qualities abound in this genre.

Starting points

- **Thinking about giants.** Ask each child to draw their version of a giant. Compare them and discuss. How many drew male giants? Why? Where does s/he live? What sort of person is s/he? What does s/he do? eat? talk like? walk like? Ask some 'What if...' questions in relation to giants, e.g. What would you do if the giant...? What would the giant say if...? Ask children to talk about giants they have met in stories. Read about some, such as in *Jack and the Beanstalk*. Brainstorm and write down appropriate giant-related words on a board.
- **Making it come alive.** Read together the introduction to the story. Act it out. Practise walking like a giant and saying his words in a deep angry voice. The children are playing in the garden and are suddenly confronted by the giant. How would they feel? How would they have felt about not being able to play in the giant's garden again? What would their view of the giant be? Imagine how he looked to them. What would they say to each other?

Activities

- **The Giant.** Discuss what the children think of the giant. Does he fit the typical stereotype? Ask the children to make up their own name for him and attempt writing a description of him. Compare and discuss. Draw some huge speech bubbles and fill them with the sorts of things the giant might have said about children. Why was he so miserable, selfish and unhappy? Try to imagine some of his past experiences that could have made him this way.
- **House and garden.** Think about where the giant would live. What would this be like? We read a little about the giant's garden. What made it so fascinating? How would the children have felt about not being able to play in the giant's garden? What would their view of the giant be? Imagine how he looked to them. How would they feel?
- **Developing the story.** In small groups, brainstorm as many different ways as possible that the story could develop. Share some of these together as a class. Choose one and finish the story. This could be attempted individually or as a small group story. It could first be written in a mini-comic strip format; or ideas could be jotted down in note form, either randomly or more systematically as a flow diagram; or writing could follow straight on from the class discussion.
- Suppose the children decided that the giant was miserable because he was lonely and was not very good at forming relationships. How could they make contact with him? Suggest children write a letter. What sort of things would they say?
- How would the children pay the giant back for being so unkind?
- Perhaps the giant's actions would make the children want to play in the garden even more. What strategies would they use to avoid him? What scrapes would they get into?

Follow-up ideas

- **Other possibilities.** This approach opens up a whole range of possibilities for writing in which fairytale-type characters appear in modern settings.
  - The Day the Dragon came to School
  - The Ghost in the Attic
  - The Genie in the Hot Water Bottle
  - The Witch who came to Tea, etc.
- **Role reversal.** With older children you can have fun turning things on their heads and making up scenarios in which the characters break out of their accepted stereotypes: the fairy godmother who turns villain; the gentle giant; the ghost who was afraid of the dark.

Trespassers Will Be Eaten!

Every afternoon on their way home from school, the children went to play in the Giant's garden, whenever he was not there.

It was a lovely large garden, with long grass to hide in, a pond to throw pebbles into and tall trees to climb. The brightly coloured birds sat on the trees and sang so sweetly that the children would sometimes stop their games and stand and listen to them. It was a lovely place to play.

Once the giant had been visiting his friend, a long way away and had stayed with him for seven months. But then he came back unexpectedly. When he arrived he saw the children playing in his garden. He was angry and cried out in such a gruff voice that the children ran away terrified. The giant decided that he did not want children playing in his garden so he built a high wall all around it and put up a notice-board.

BEWARE -

TRESPASSERS WILL BE EATEN!

Think of a name for the giant: _____

Now describe him. _____

_____

_____

_____

_____

_____

_____

Continue over the page

DIY Fairy Stories - Ideas Page

Starting points

- **Characters in fairy stories.** Read or retell a typical fairy story.
- **Discuss the main characters.** What were they like? What sort of things did they do? Which ones did the children like/dislike? Ask the children to explain their likes/dislikes. Draw both favourite and most disliked characters. Look together at the pictures. Comment on how well children think the pictures capture the characters.
- **Goodies and baddies.** Discuss how fairy stories often have fairly well-defined 'goodies' and 'baddies'. Try to categorise the characters.
- **Places in fairy stories.** Ask the children to identify a few of the key places where the action takes place in the story you shared together, e.g. in the woods, at the palace.

Activities

- **Draw the missing character.** Look at the character cards and explain that these are the sorts of characters that are often found in fairy stories. Discuss what other characters might also be found. Each child could then choose another character and draw and label it in the empty frame.
- **Character stereotypes.** Look at one of the characters together, e.g. the dragon. What words come to mind when thinking about dragons? Brainstorm and list some describing words and phrases on the board, e.g. scaly, huge, flappy wings, staring eyes, hot breath, sharp teeth and claws. Ask the children in pairs or small groups to do the same with the other characters. Afterwards, suggest some of the groups share their thoughts and discuss some of the more exciting words. What sorts of things do dragons do? What do they eat? Where do they live? What do they say? How do they behave?
- **Character profiles.** Work in pairs. Ask children to choose one character to discuss. Think about things like appearance, background details, personality and qualities, likes, dislikes, dreams or wishes. Let the children share some of their descriptions. They could be word-processed or typed up and displayed around the room underneath the appropriate pictures. Descriptions of the same characters could be compared and discussed, attention being drawn to the way different people see different characters.
- **Draw the missing place.** Look at the setting cards and discuss the sorts of places commonly found in fairy stories. Ask the children to draw another place they can each think of in the blank frame.
- **Discuss each place.** Who would be found there? Ask children to describe what they think these places are like. Would it make a difference if they were describing the place at night? if they were all alone in the place? if it was at different times of the year? What sort of things might happen at each place?

Follow-up ideas

Writing a fairy story. Cut out the character and setting cards.
- Working in small groups, ask the children to select three characters (making sure that they choose at least one 'goody' and one 'baddy', including one of the characters that they wrote a profile of). Also ask them to choose places where they want the action to take place.
- Suggest some possible themes for a story: the 'goody' has something that the 'baddy' wants to steal; the 'baddy' is jealous of the 'goody' and wants to hurt him or her.
- Ask the children to share story-line ideas, which must include the chosen characters and places. Suggest that they think of the story in three sections:
    - *The beginning* (Once upon a time ... introduction of characters and scene); *the middle* (a turning point to get the action moving) *the end* (a problem, or unusual event). Attempts to resolve it (the story must have a clear outcome). Draw a sequence of pictures showing the story outline.
- Write the stories, read them to one another and discuss.

Fairy Stories

CHARACTER CARDS

Princess	Wicked Queen	Giant
Magic Horse	Dragon	

SETTING CARDS

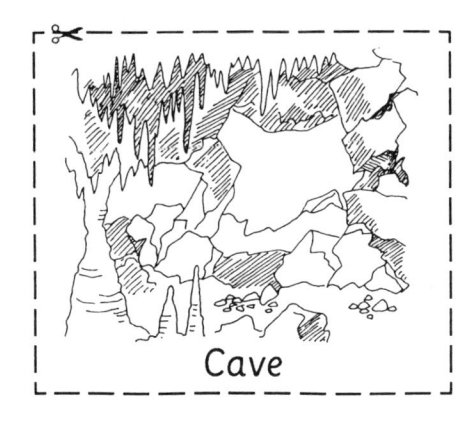

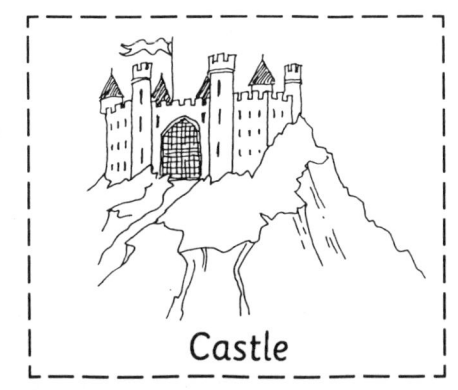

Cave	Woods	Palace
Castle	Mountain	

Dreamtime - Ideas Page

Background

Different cultures have myths and stories embodying traditional beliefs, e.g. Greek and Norse legends and myths. In these, the normal laws of nature are relatively flexible and unformulated - anything can, and frequently does, happen. These provide a wonderful source of stories to thrill the imagination and stimulate writing opportunities. This activity is based on *Dreamtime*, an Australian aboriginal creation story. Before embarking on the activities, explain the origin of the story to the children.

Activities

- **Using prediction and building the story.** Using prediction and studying a text in the following way has many benefits:
  - It encourages interaction with the text.
  - It gradually gives children the feeling for the particular genre of story being studied.
  - It encourages children to create ideas for stories collectively and to become aware of other possibilities.
  - It enables different aspects to be focused on, e.g. characters, style.
- Cut the story sheets into strips. Work in pairs or small groups.
- Discuss and study the story strips one at a time.
- Read the relevant section to the class or ask children to read it in groups. Discuss and follow up anything of interest in each section, e.g. you could ask the children to use their imagination to describe the Rainbow Serpent. What did it look like? How did it move? How big was it? What clues are there in the text to help?
- After this, ask each group to talk about what they think will happen next. Share their thoughts with the class and discuss their suggestions.
- Gradually, as each strip is dealt with, the story will build up. This process may take some time, even spanning one or more lessons depending on how much discussion ensues. Remember to re-tell the story so far, or ask the children to do so, every time a new section is given out.

Follow up ideas

- **Developing the story.** There are several possible ways for developing the story in writing:
- **The meeting.** Ask the children to imagine what the mass meeting of all the animals would have been like. Who would have been there? How would it have been conducted? How would order have been kept? What sort of things might have been said and done? What would the outcome have been?
- **Rules and laws.** Discuss how important it is for us to have rules - at home, in school, in society. Think about some - why they are there, who enforces and judges them, what happens when they are broken? Think of rules for particular creatures, e.g. make up some rules for koalas, frogs, kangaroos, or for snakes.
- **How things were formed.** Re-read the section about how rivers, lakes and seas were formed. Consider how other things like the sun, sky, moon, stars, rain, snow, wind, mountains, rocks, trees, fruit and vegetables were formed.
- **Distinctive animal characteristics.** Giraffes have long necks, elephants have trunks, skunks have an unpleasant smell, frogs and toads hop. Discuss together how some of these animals might have developed these characteristics. Remember that within this genre anything is possible! Encourage creative and divergent responses. Ask children to work in pairs and make up their own story. Make up a class book on the theme.
- **Human beings.** The section of *Dreamtime* used in this book only talks about animals. Later, the original story describes how human beings came on to the scene. Encourage the children to use their imagination and give their ideas on how this might have happened.
- Look at and read together some myths and legends from the past, as a stimulus for discussion and further writing.
- Read the biblical view of creation from a children's Bible. Discuss similarities and differences with *Dreamtime*.

Dreamtime

1) In Dreamtime, at the beginning of the world, it was dark. Nothing grew. Nothing moved. All the birds, animals and reptiles were asleep under the ground.

2) One day the Rainbow Serpent woke up and began to look around. Wherever she crawled she left a winding track. Wherever she slept she left a huge hollow in the ground.

3) After a while it became lonely so the Rainbow Serpent decided to wake up the other creatures. The big-bellied frogs were the first to emerge. Their stomachs were full of water they had stored.

4) The frogs looked so funny that the Rainbow Serpent tickled them with her tongue. They laughed so much that all the water inside them started to rush out. It filled the tracks and hollows left by the Rainbow Serpent. This is how the lakes, rivers and seas were first formed.

5) After all the creatures had woken up and come out from under the ground, they all lived happily together. But then things started to go wrong and they began to argue and fight.

6) Rainbow Serpent could stand it no longer. She decided that they all needed some laws to help them live together in peace. She called all the creatures together.

Sequencing and Predicting - Ideas Page

Background

In all stories something happens, there is some action or a chain of events (plot). We can focus on events, actions or happenings as a way into storytelling.

Starting points

- A simple way to introduce a sequence of events to children is to ask them to put a jumbled set of pictures or sentences in order, e.g. making a sandwich, washing the dog, going to school. Alternatively they could be asked to write the explanation themselves (or give them orally). The tasks could become increasingly difficult as the children get older, e.g. explaining the rules of a game or sport.

Activities

Using picture sequences to support story-telling.
- Cut up and give out the set of pictures from the top half of the activity page. In pairs, the children should discuss and work out a story by putting them in a particular order. Discuss any different outcomes. There is no right or wrong answer. Now ask each pair to flesh out and make up a story based on the pictures. Share the different stories.
- More difficult sequences can be devised, containing a greater number of pictures. To make it more interesting, a key picture, e.g. from the beginning, middle or end, can be withheld and the children work out what is missing. Sentences rather than pictures can be used and the same approach adopted. (See *Dreamtime* on page 31.)
- **Retelling stories orally or in pictures.**
(See 'Remembering and Retelling Stories' page 6 for further ideas.)
Encouraging children to retell stories they have heard, read or seen in their own words is a helpful way of ensuring they identify key events in their correct sequence. Occasionally it is also worthwhile asking them to retell the story in pictures. You could provide a comic strip frame or set of blank picture frames. They could use as many or as few as they wanted, or limits could be imposed. Simple captions could be added or dialogue written if desired.
- **Predicting.** Using a picture (like the one on the bottom half of the page) containing plenty of action can help children set a context for story-writing. Talk about what is actually happening. Discuss what might have just happened and what they think is going to happen next.

Follow-up Ideas

- **Cliffhangers.** Talk about 'cliffhangers' and the way TV series often cut the action at a critical point. Discuss something they are watching at the moment and predict how they think the story will continue. As a story is being read, stop from time to time and ask children to guess what happens next. Use this strategy as a basis for developing story-writing. Give the children a passage (made up like the one on page 27, or from a story book). In groups ask them to talk about the characters, the setting, what is happening and how they think the story will progress.
As they become more proficient at this idea give them shorter texts as the beginning of a story (see page 35), or as the middle or endings. The degree of support needed will depend on the children's ages and abilities.

Picture Story Sequencing

Prediction using pictures

Stimulating Ideas - Ideas Page

Background

The events that form the basis of children's writing may be fairly everyday occurrences enabling children to respond using their own personal experiences, e.g. breaking a promise, having an argument; they may be somewhat unusual, requiring children to use their knowledge, experience and imagination, e.g. a flood, being kidnapped; or the events may be highly unlikely, requiring the use of considerable imagination, e.g. a UFO landing in the back garden!

Starting points

- The 'Events' Starter web (below) may be used as a resource of story starter ideas for the teacher to use and develop as appropriate. Alternatively it could be used as a resource for children, to help stimulate ideas when they plan a story. If used in this way it would be best for children to work collaboratively. Use the Stimulating Ideas sheet (on page 35) to get children started. Then move on to the Starter web technique.
- Other 'Events' Starter Webs could be created, e.g. for fairy stories, for tales of times gone by, for science fiction stories, for westerns or animal stories.

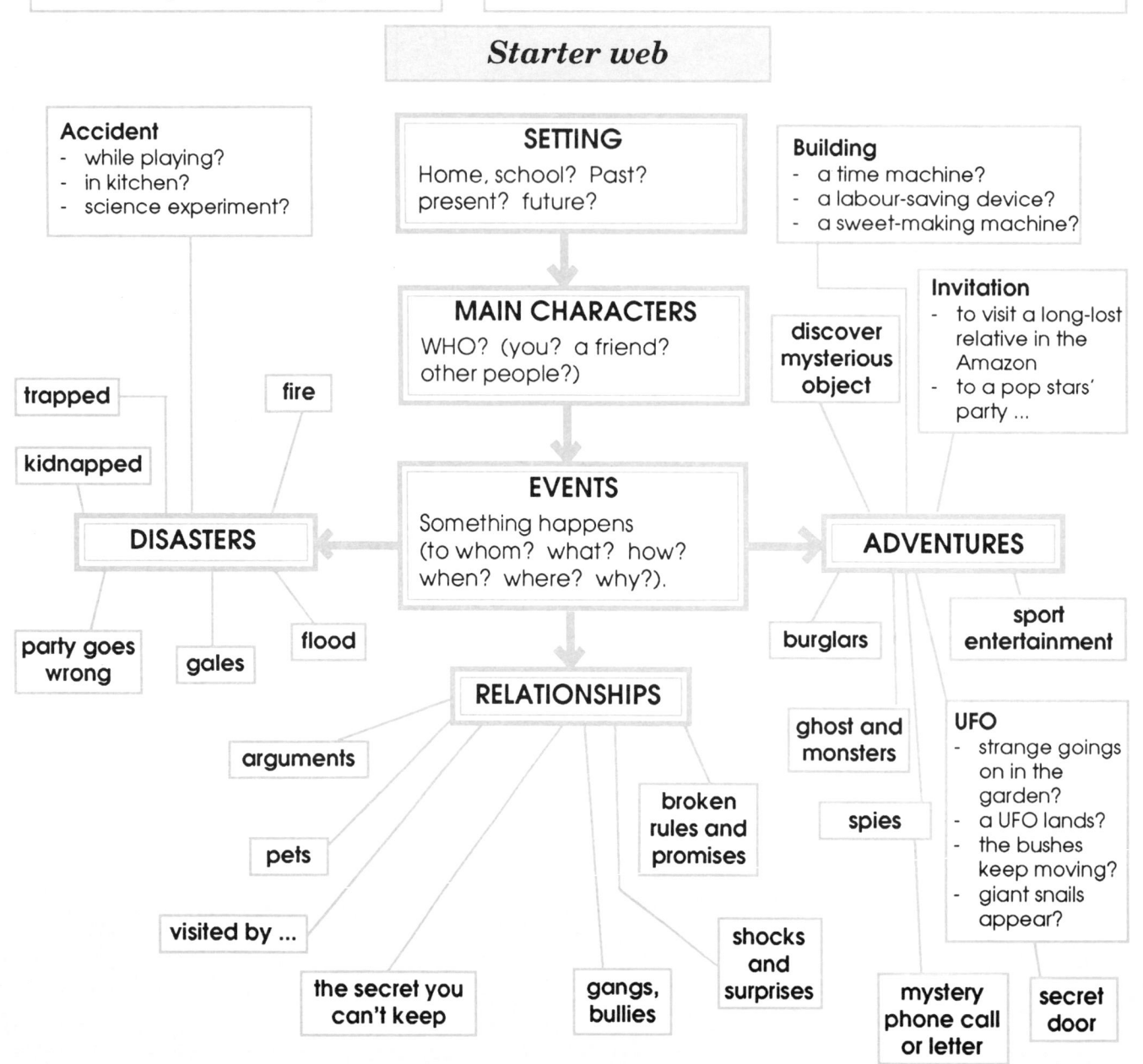

Starter web

Accident
- while playing?
- in kitchen?
- science experiment?

SETTING
Home, school? Past? present? future?

Building
- a time machine?
- a labour-saving device?
- a sweet-making machine?

MAIN CHARACTERS
WHO? (you? a friend? other people?)

Invitation
- to visit a long-lost relative in the Amazon
- to a pop stars' party ...

discover mysterious object

trapped

fire

kidnapped

EVENTS
Something happens (to whom? what? how? when? where? why?).

DISASTERS

ADVENTURES

party goes wrong

gales

flood

burglars

sport entertainment

RELATIONSHIPS

ghost and monsters

UFO
- strange goings on in the garden?
- a UFO lands?
- the bushes keep moving?
- giant snails appear?

arguments

spies

pets

broken rules and promises

visited by ...

shocks and surprises

the secret you can't keep

gangs, bullies

mystery phone call or letter

secret door

IDEAS BANK - Telling Stories F5186 © Folens.

Stimulating Ideas

A SHOCK FOR SHIVA ON PLANET VULCAN

Explorer 2 touched down on Planet Vulcan. The crew switched on the scanner and looked out at the rocky landscape.

'It looks pretty unfriendly to me,' whispered Shiva. She clutched her transformer tightly.

Shiva was on Planet Vulcan to undertake some scientific experiments. The rest of the crew were going to remain on board. She carried the transformer in case of emergencies. There was enough power in it to give her an extra charge of superhuman power to help her get out of difficulties.

Her friends patted her on the back and wished her luck as she stepped down onto the surface of Planet Vulcan. Shiva gave a slight shudder as she set off towards the mountains in the distance. She could not help feeling she was being watched.

Suddenly, out of nowhere, a huge hairy alien hand appeared. Shiva's heart pounded. There was nowhere to run. She grasped the transformer. She pressed the switch and immediately felt a surge of power racing through her body ...

Some Story Starters

Everyone seemed to have a pet except for Winston. Sarah had a cat, Shirin had a snappy little poodle, Tom had a gerbil that looked like a fur ball. Winston decided it was time he had a pet.

It all started the day the Browns went for a picnic. They were just sitting down, munching their sandwiches and crisps, when Emma spotted something gleaming in the bushes.

This is the story of Barney, the boy who collected marbles. You may think this is not very unusual, but you would be wrong! One morning Barney discovered there was something strange about his marble collection.

Under the Manhole Cover! - Ideas Page

Starting points

- **Mysterious Creatures**
  Discuss the claims made by some people that creatures we have never yet seen exist. What do the children know of the Loch Ness Monster and the Abominable Snowman? Do they really exist? Talk about the exploration of the ocean depths and outer space and the possibility of other, as yet undiscovered and un-documented, life forms. Perhaps children could draw what they think the Abominable Snowman looks like. This could be a stimulus to an 'In search of the Yeti'-type adventure story in its own right.

Activities

- **Sequence the pictures.** Cut up the pictures. Explain that they tell the beginning of a story. In pairs, arrange the pictures so that they make sense. Give the characters names. Ask the children to discuss what they think is happening. What would the characters be saying? Elaborate on the information given, e.g. talk about characters, their feelings and how they react. Share ideas together as a class.
- **Finish the story.** In pairs, discuss how the story might finish. Who else might be involved? How will it end? Will it be a happy ending? Will something terrible go wrong? The story could be recorded in strip cartoon form with speech bubbles, written or tape-recorded.

Follow-up ideas

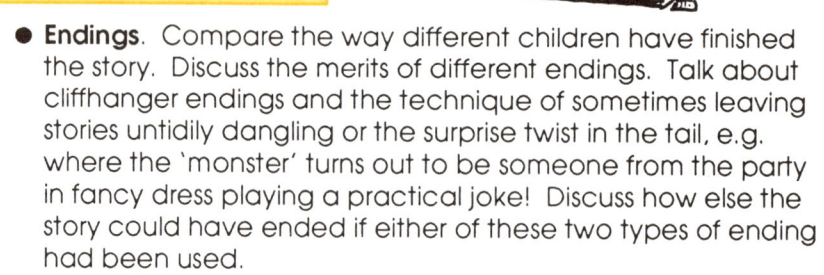

- **Endings.** Compare the way different children have finished the story. Discuss the merits of different endings. Talk about cliffhanger endings and the technique of sometimes leaving stories untidily dangling or the surprise twist in the tail, e.g. where the 'monster' turns out to be someone from the party in fancy dress playing a practical joke! Discuss how else the story could have ended if either of these two types of ending had been used.
- **Beginnings.** No explanation is offered as to how what is under the manhole cover came to be there. Create a good beginning to the story.
- **Animal research.** Discuss the idea of animal research and the possible reasons for biological experimentation, e.g. to produce a bee with greater honey-making potential. Introduce the idea of producing hybrid creatures, e.g. by crossing a lion with a tiger. Brainstorm, and perhaps draw, some unusual combinations.
- **Science fiction stories.** Below are some possible starting points, to provide children with the ideas for plots, to develop into stories:
  Things that could go wrong. For example:
  - a mix-up in the laboratory (too strong an electrical charge, incorrect proportions of chemicals injected).
  - Unforeseen circumstances (something the scientists overlook, e.g. the effect of sunlight; the creation behaves differently than expected, rebels against being controlled and develops a mind of its own; radioactive leak affects previously normal species, e.g. giant spiders; nuclear explosion creates abnormal conditions; pollution affects creature's development).
  - Scientists set out to create a monster for their own purpose, e.g. to rule the world (Frankenstein, robot, Bionic Man) with disastrous effects.
  Other possible scenarios:
  - Invasion by creatures from outer space (well-intentioned ET-types and more threatening sorts).
  - Ocean depths and loch investigations.
  - Himalayan monsters.
  - Prehistoric beings which have lain dormant for millions of years.

Under the Manhole Cover!

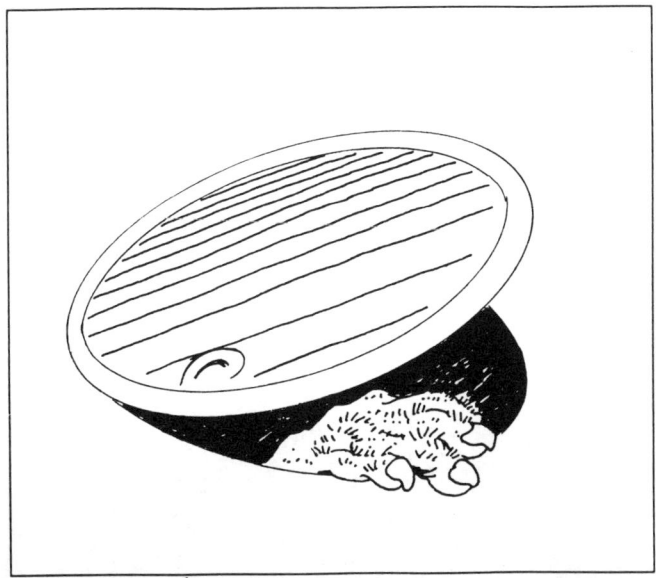

Daring Deeds at Drakensberg - Ideas Page

Starting points

- Classic children's stories like the *Narnia Chronicles* by C. S. Lewis are built around storylines in which good and evil forces are pitted against each other. *Daring Deeds at Drakensberg* presents a structure for creating an adventure story using the same type of theme.
- This idea offers possibilities for collaborative writing in pairs or small groups. It is suggested that the children initially tackle the set of supported writing tasks on this page. If the idea catches the children's imagination, there is scope for developing it into an extended story in chapter form, using the ideas on page 40.

Activities

Set the scene

- Provide each pair or small group with a copy of the photocopiable activity sheet. Give the following information, referring to sections of the sheet as you do:

  The evil Duke of Doom lives in the fortified and menacing Drakensberg Castle high in the snow-covered mountains. He has long plotted to plunder the wealth of peaceful Shalomnia. He has snatched Princess Starlight, the King of Shalomnia's daughter and is holding her to ransom. King Solomon of Shalomnia has sent a rescue party to rescue her and has appointed you as leader. Your companions on this mission are:

  Sterling the Warrior. He is one of the King's most trusted and brave soldiers. He carries a sword said to have magical qualities. It is claimed that whoever holds the sword will never be defeated.

  Sapphire the Seer. She is a good friend of the Princess. She has special visionary powers. One stare from her hypnotic eyes can immobilise people and creatures temporarily. Amazingly, she can see in the dark and see through solid objects.

  Spright the Dwarf. Though short and stocky, Spright is immensely strong. He is an excellent climber. He has an intimate knowledge of the area and its inhabitants. He is able to communicate with most creatures.

- If desired the children could make up another member of the rescue party.

  So far, the children have succeeded in breaking into the castle, locating and freeing the Princess from the dungeons. The children surprised the soldier guarding the Princess and have bound and gagged him, and locked him in one of the dungeons.

Pose the problems

- Children now have to escape from Drakensberg Castle. In doing so children must:
  - collect enough food for the journey home (about three days)
  - sabotage the weapons store
  - escape without the alarm being raised
  - find a way of slowing down any possible pursuit.

Give the children a number of problems to solve. Choose from the above, or add to the list as appropriate.

Follow-up ideas

- **Discuss and write.** In their groups, children should:
  - Look carefully at the plan of the castle basement and consider what they have to do. Discuss the problems within the castle, situations that might arise and how they would deal with them.
  - Discuss possible problems once outside.
  - Formulate, consider and discuss a plan of action.
    At this point an additional possibility is for the groups to share together their thoughts and plans and to discuss their relative merits and disadvantages. The children can learn from each other's ideas and make changes to their own if desired.
    Write a story about how they escape from the castle.

Daring Deeds at Drakensberg

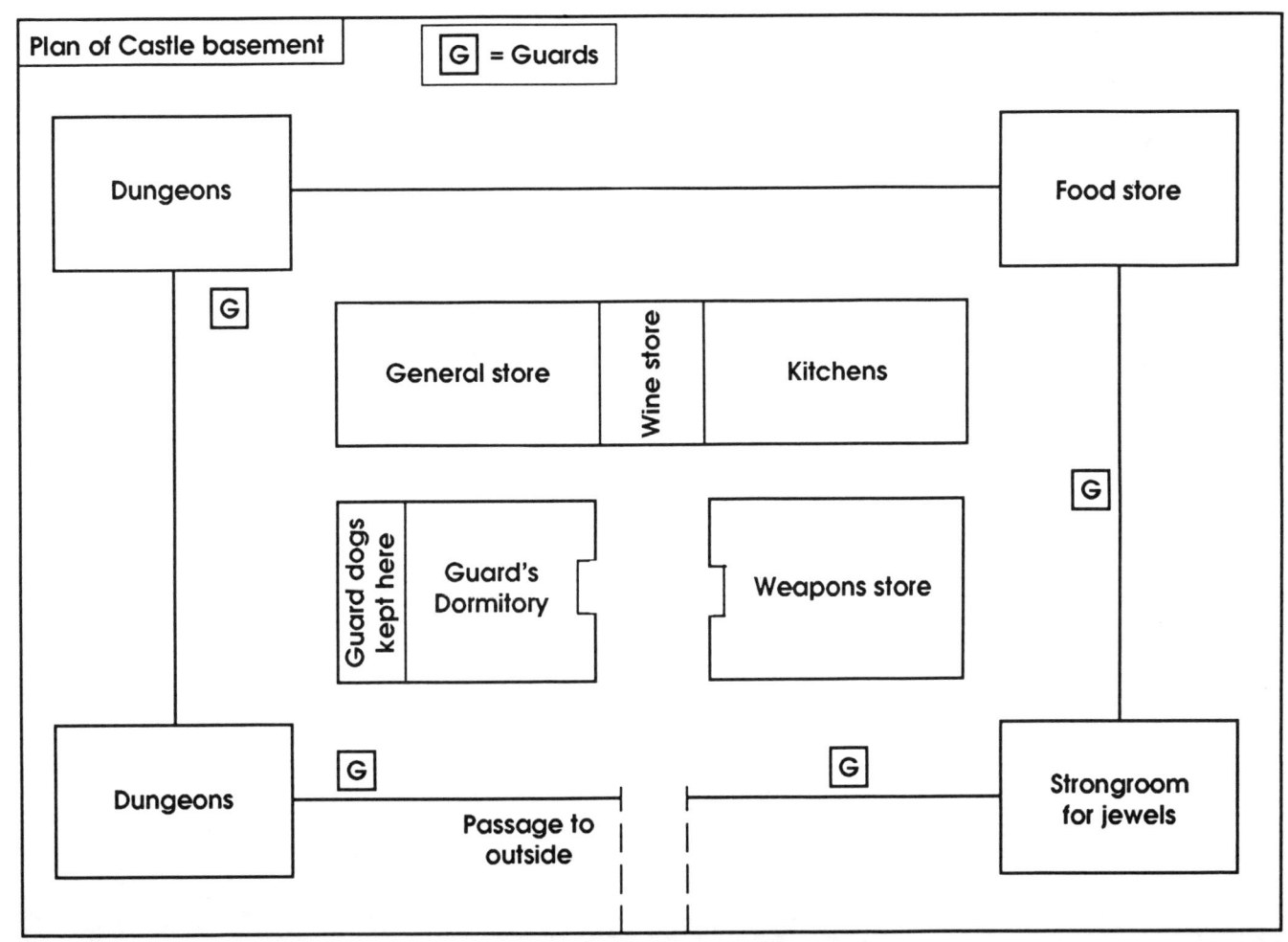

MAP

Drakensberg Castle
Drakensberg Mountains
River Styx
Forest of Zendor
Shalomnia

Princess Starlight

Sapphire the Seer

Sterling the Warrior

Spright the Dwarf

Plan of Castle basement

G = Guards

- Dungeons
- Food store
- General store
- Wine store
- Kitchens
- Guard dogs kept here
- Guard's Dormitory
- Weapons store
- Dungeons
- Passage to outside
- Strongroom for jewels

© Folens.   IDEAS BANK - Telling Stories F5186

Extending the Story - Ideas Page

Starting points

Encourage children to write longer stories by creating structured writing opportunities, forming more chapters in the adventure. Use each picture on the activity sheet as a stimulus for separate chapters. Set the scene each time and pose several possible scenarios. The class could collectively be involved in thinking about more possibilities. Each group could then create and share their plans for stories and written outcomes.

Activities

In the Mountains
- **Set the scene**
  The group succeeds in escaping but had not anticipated the atrocious weather conditions. It is night, the wind is howling and thick snow is falling. The ledge down the cliff face is narrow, crumbling and treacherous.
- **Pose the problems**
  - One of the group stumbles, slips and falls down the cliff.
  - There is an avalanche.
  - The Duke of Doom gives chase. He has a secret weapon.
  - Other possibilities.
- **Discuss and write**
  How do the group manage to get down the mountain safely?

Crossing the river
- **Set the scene**
  At last the group reaches the river. It is swollen and running fast. It is too cold and too far to the other side to chance swimming. The mountains of Drakensberg are behind you. Shalomnia lies across the river ahead. The group must get to the other side.
- **Pose the problems**
  - There is no bridge and the boat has disappeared.
  - On the way across a sudden squall hits the group and throws everyone into the water.
  - The serpent of the Styx rears its ugly head!
  - Other possibilities.
- **Discuss and write**
  How do the group manage to get across the river safely?

Facing the forest
- **Set the scene**
  Undaunted by these adventures the group faces the last barrier between them and home - the fearsome Forest of Zendor! Dusk is falling. The food is fast running out. The group must find its way through this dark and dangerous forest.
- **Pose the problems**
  - The Princess is exhausted by now. Someone has to carry her.
  - The forest is full of traps set by Grigor the Gremlin.
  - The forest creatures are far from friendly.
  - The forest floor is boggy in places. Sinking sands abound.
  - Other possibilities.
- **Discuss and write**
  Tell the story of the journey through the forest.

Follow-up ideas

- Other possible chapters could be:
  - The celebrations and the welcome home.
  - Chapter 1 telling some of the events that led up to where we began.
  - Many of the episodes lend themselves to being made into tape-recorded plays, using a narrator, sound effects and music.
  - Make a frieze or 'tapestry' (like the Bayeux Tapestry) telling the story.
  - In art, make some life-size pictures of the characters and incorporate their words in speech bubbles.
- The longer story could be turned into a book-making opportunity. It could be word-processed, illustrated and 'published' for the rest of the class and others to read.

Extending the Story

In the mountains

Crossing the river

Facing the forest

Supporting the Writing Process - Ideas Page

Background

- Throughout this book, children are encouraged to reflect on different aspects of the writing process. The following sheets (pages 43-47) draw it all together and make the process more explicit. The sheets and checklists act as *aides mémoires* to help guide and structure children's thinking about the writing process.
- The sheets provide comprehensive coverage of all the steps in the process BUT should be used flexibly and selectively. Writers do not necessarily always use every step. Sometimes an alternative approach may be appropriate. Also, to expect every child to follow a set pattern intensively on every writing occasion would be to court disaster and to kill motivation and enjoyment.
However, from time to time using these ideas can encourage reflection and a greater appreciation and understanding of writing, as well as producing better organised, planned and executed writing.

Starting points

- Children may be given as many or as few of the sheets as appropriate, depending on the teaching objectives. When to use them depends very much on the teacher's discretion and the needs of the children.
- Regular teacher/child writing conferences are recommended, in order that specific pieces of work may, from time to time, be discussed in detail. The sheets and checklists are useful for reference. Perhaps enlarged copies could be made for the wall or notice-board. Children could paste relevant sheets inside the covers of their exercise books for reference.
NB When writing a piece which is intended as a first draft, it is sometimes helpful to suggest writing on every other line or using one side of each double page of the exercise book, leaving the other line or side blank to allow for editing.

Activities

- **Steps to Becoming a Real Author.** This provides a comprehensive overview of the steps involved in the writing process.
- **Story-Planning Checklist.** This sets out and draws together all the key elements in stories, providing an invaluable list to help children think through their ideas in the early stages of planning.
- **Story-Planning Wheel.** This is a helpful device, allowing children to organise their notes and thoughts and providing a logical structure for them. Other devices like scatter webs may be used.
- **Reviewing Checklist.** As the checklist mentions, this stage of the process is best undertaken with others (teacher or partners). The checklist supports structured discussion about the important elements of story-writing.
- **Editing Checklist.** After the main redrafting process, this checklist helps children focus on fine-tuning and surface structures and moves towards deciding about issues of effective presentation.

Steps to Becoming a Real Author

1 PUBLISHING

- Decide in what form you want your story to be published. A book? on paper?
- Think about any illustrations you want.
- Write it out in your best handwriting or word process it. Illustrate it.

EDITING

- Now check it through for silly, small mistakes in spelling or punctuation.
- Use your Editing Checklist to help.
- Ask someone else to check your work too (a friend or your teacher).

REVIEWING

- Read your story. Share it with someone else. Discuss it together.
- Use your Reviewing Checklist to help.
- Make any changes you need to.
- You can cross out parts, add things or move words or sentences about.

4 DRAFTING

- Write the first draft of your story in rough.
- Write on paper or use a word processor.

5 PLANNING

- Decide what you want your story to be about.
- Use the Story Planning Checklist and personal Story Planning Wheel to help.
- Discuss your ideas with others.

Story Planning Checklist

TYPE OF STORY
- What sort of story do you want to write?
  - Adventure?
  - Mystery?
  - Animal?
  - True to life?
  - Imaginary?
  - Funny?
  - Other?

SETTING
- When will the story take place?
  - In the present?
  - In the future?
  - In the past?
- Where will it take place?
  - In a 'real' setting, e.g. town, country, castle, house?
  - In an imaginary setting, e.g. another planet?

CHARACTERS
- Who will the main characters be?
- Will the characters be:
  - human, e.g. people you know, made-up characters?
  - animals?
  - other?
- What will the characters be like?
  - Their appearance?
  - Their personalities (their qualities, things they say and do)?

PLOT
- How will the story begin?
- What sorts of things will happen in the story?
- How will the story end?
  - Will it have a clear ending?
  - Will the ending be happy? sad? exciting? mysterious? something else?
  - Will it leave the reader wanting to know more?

Use your Story Planning Wheel to make some notes before you begin.

Story Planning Wheel

Name _____ Story title _____

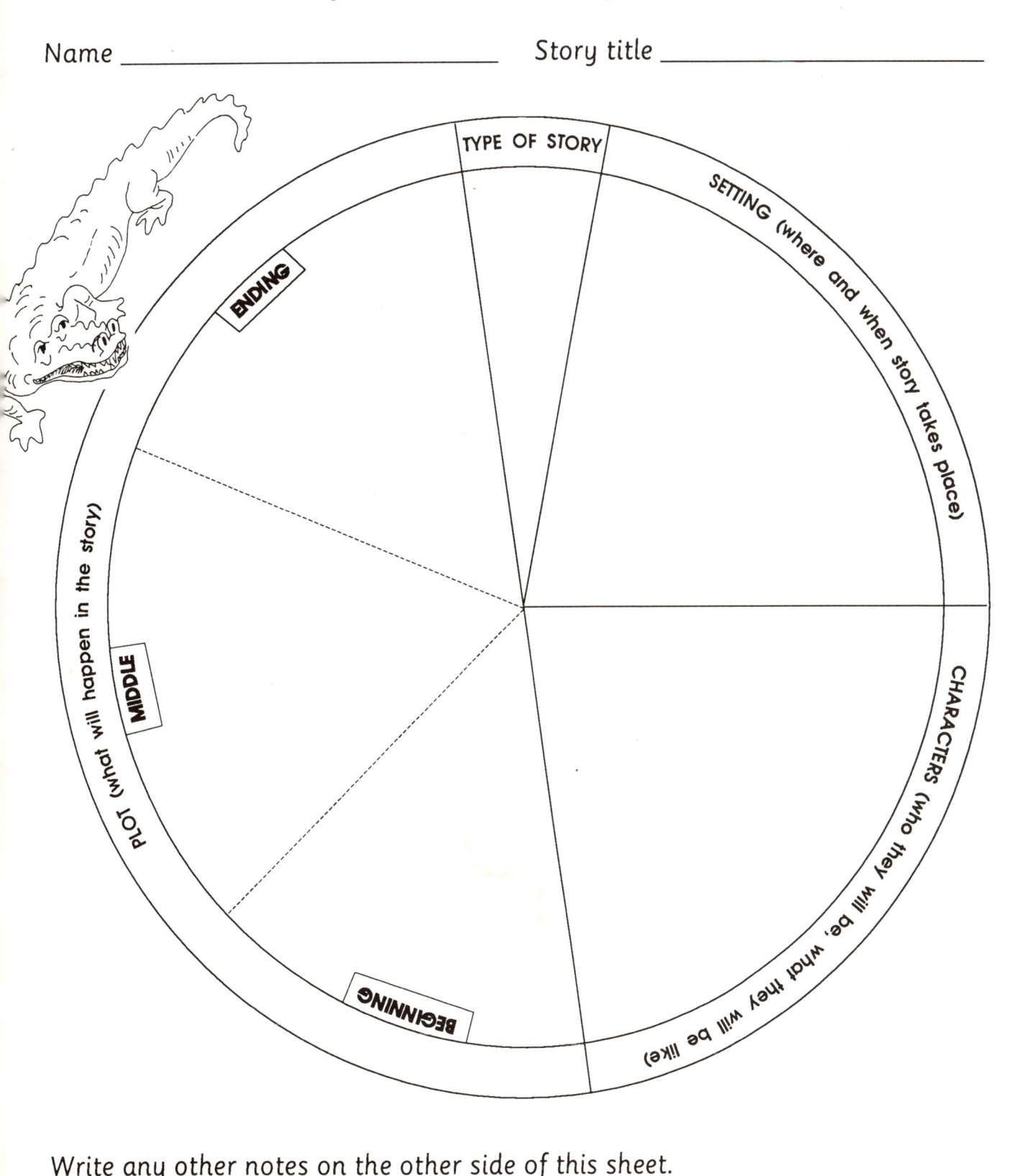

TYPE OF STORY

SETTING (where and when story takes place)

CHARACTERS (who they will be, what they will be like)

BEGINNING

PLOT (what will happen in the story)

MIDDLE

ENDING

Write any other notes on the other side of this sheet.

Now you are ready to write the first draft of your story.

© Folens IDEAS BANK - Telling Stories F5186

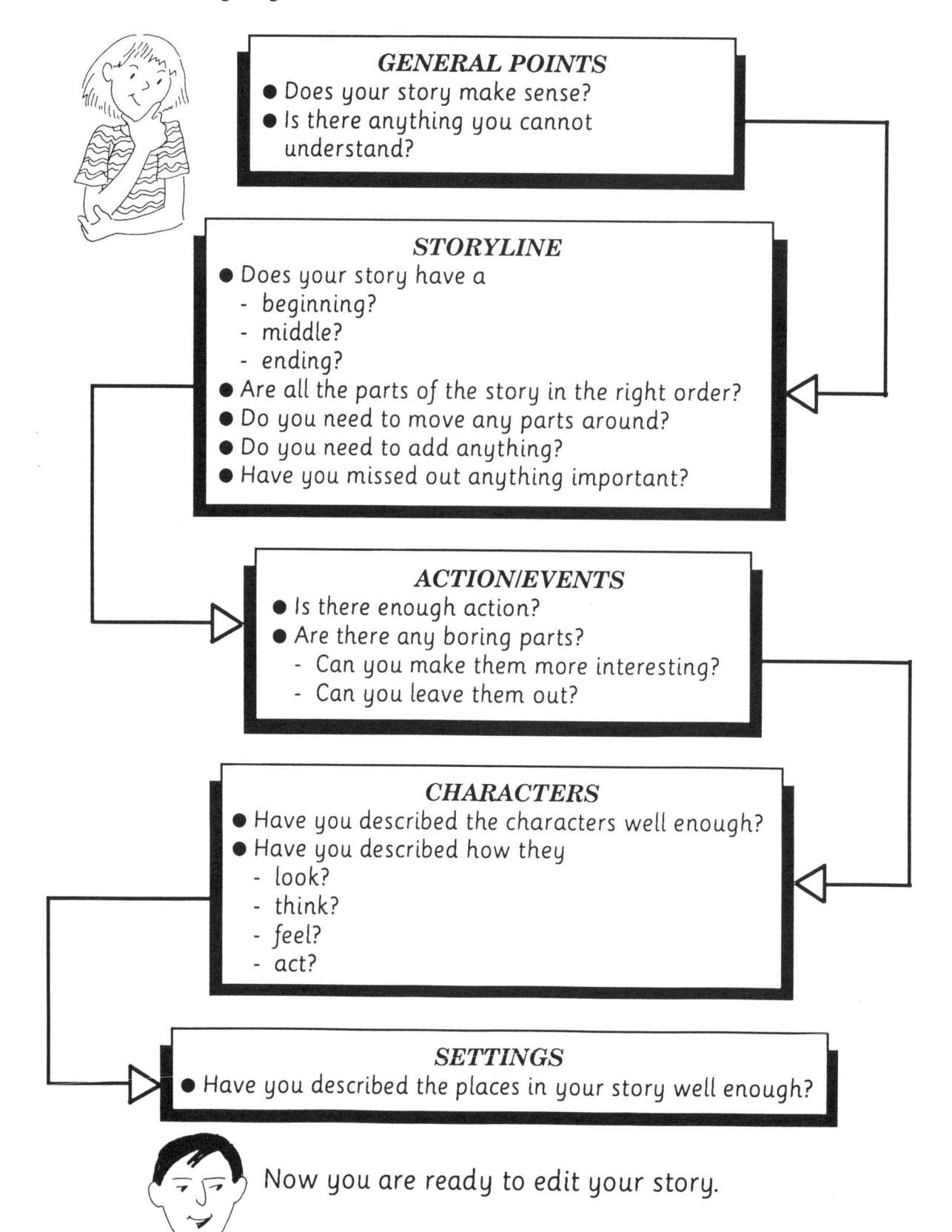

Reviewing Checklist

When you have finished the first draft of your story read it through. Use the Checklist to help you talk about your story.
Make all the changes you need.

GENERAL POINTS
- Does your story make sense?
- Is there anything you cannot understand?

STORYLINE
- Does your story have a
  - beginning?
  - middle?
  - ending?
- Are all the parts of the story in the right order?
- Do you need to move any parts around?
- Do you need to add anything?
- Have you missed out anything important?

ACTION/EVENTS
- Is there enough action?
- Are there any boring parts?
  - Can you make them more interesting?
  - Can you leave them out?

CHARACTERS
- Have you described the characters well enough?
- Have you described how they
  - look?
  - think?
  - feel?
  - act?

SETTINGS
- Have you described the places in your story well enough?

Now you are ready to edit your story.

IDEAS BANK - Telling Stories F5186   © Folens.

Editing Checklist

When you have reviewed your story read it through. Use the Checklist to help you think about your story and check for any small changes that need to be made.

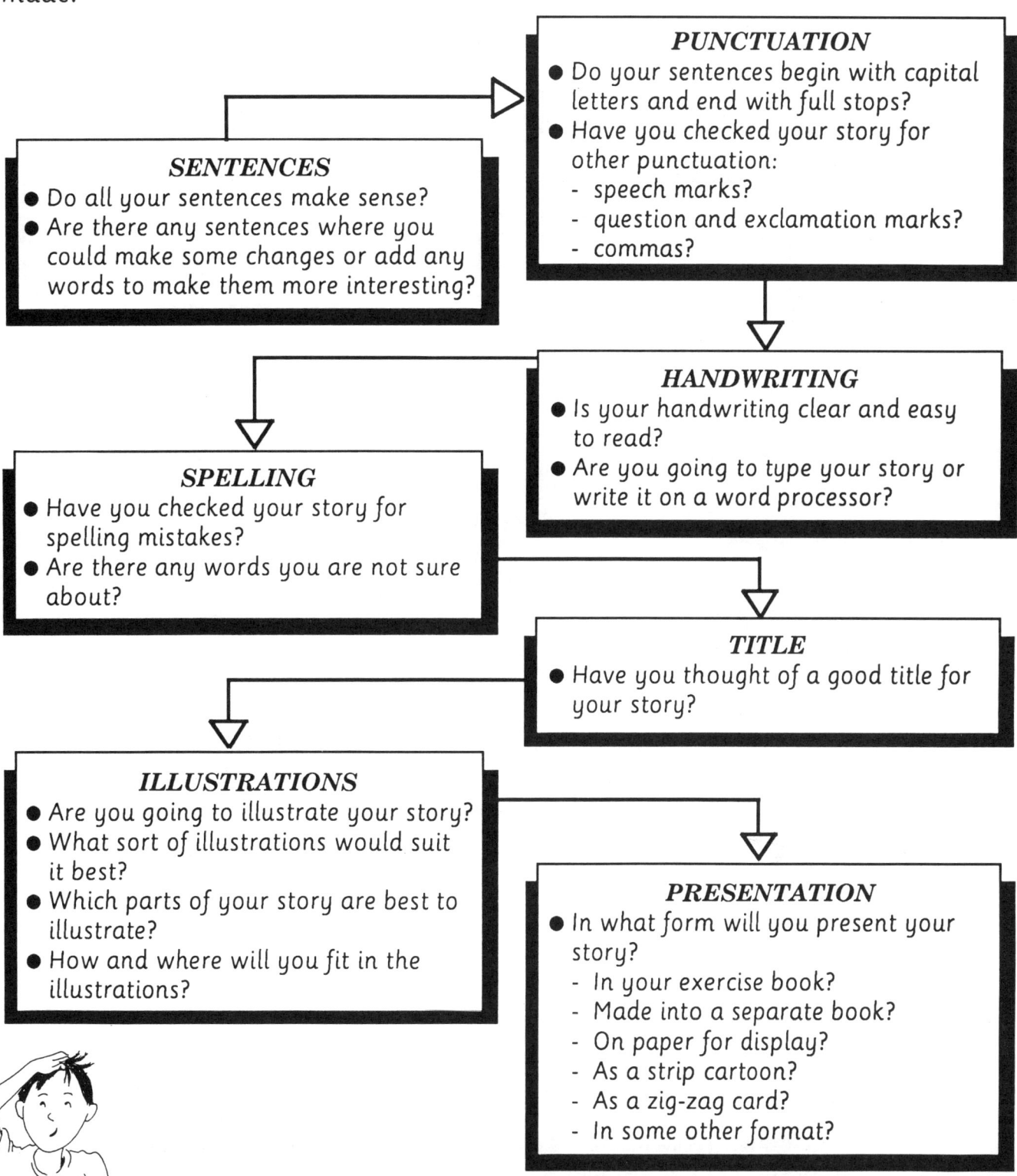

PUNCTUATION
- Do your sentences begin with capital letters and end with full stops?
- Have you checked your story for other punctuation:
  - speech marks?
  - question and exclamation marks?
  - commas?

SENTENCES
- Do all your sentences make sense?
- Are there any sentences where you could make some changes or add any words to make them more interesting?

HANDWRITING
- Is your handwriting clear and easy to read?
- Are you going to type your story or write it on a word processor?

SPELLING
- Have you checked your story for spelling mistakes?
- Are there any words you are not sure about?

TITLE
- Have you thought of a good title for your story?

ILLUSTRATIONS
- Are you going to illustrate your story?
- What sort of illustrations would suit it best?
- Which parts of your story are best to illustrate?
- How and where will you fit in the illustrations?

PRESENTATION
- In what form will you present your story?
  - In your exercise book?
  - Made into a separate book?
  - On paper for display?
  - As a strip cartoon?
  - As a zig-zag card?
  - In some other format?

Now you are ready to write the final version of your story.

© Folens. IDEAS BANK - Telling Stories F5186

Eight ways to help ...

There are hundreds of ideas in this book to enable you to develop and extend the photocopiable pages. Here are just eight ways to help you make the most of the Ideas Bank series.

1. Photocopy a page, paste on to card and laminate/cover with sticky-backed plastic to use with groups. Children can now write on the pages using water-based pens and this can be washed off.

2. Photocopy on to both sides of the paper. Put another useful activity on the back. Develop a simple filing system so others can find relevant sheets and do not duplicate them again.

3. Save the sheets - if the children do not have to cut them up as a part of the activity - and re-use. Label the sets, and keep them safely in files.

4. Make the most of group work. Children working in small groups need one sheet to discuss between them.

5. Put the sheets inside clear plastic wallets. This means the sheets are easily stored in a binder and will last longer. Children's writing can again be wiped away.

6. Use as an ideas page for yourself. Discuss issues with the class and get children to produce artwork and writing.

7. Make an overhead transparency of the page. You and your colleagues can now use the idea time and time again.

8. Ask yourself: 'Does every child in this class/group need to deal with/work through this photocopiable sheet?' If not, don't photocopy it!

© Folens.